WAR VEHICLES

VEHICLES of the IRAQ WAR

by Rebecca Love Fishkin

Consultant:
Dennis P. Mroczkowski
Colonel, U.S. Marine Corps Reserve (Retired)
Williamsburg, Virginia

CAPSTONE PRESS
a capstone imprint

Edge Books are published by Capstone Press,
1710 Roe Crest Drive, North Mankato, Minnesota 56003
www.capstonepub.com

Library of Congress Cataloging-in-Publication Data
Fishkin, Rebecca Love, 1972–
Vehicles of the Iraq War / by Rebecca Love Fishkin.
pages cm.—(Edge books. War vehicles)
Includes bibliographical references and index.
Summary: "Describes various land, air, and sea vehicles used by U.S. and Iraqi forces during the Iraq War"—Provided by publisher.
Audience: Ages 8-14.
ISBN 978-1-4296-9914-3 (library binding)
ISBN 978-1-4765-3379-7 (ebook PDF)
1. Vehicles, Military—History—21st century—Juvenile literature. 2. Iraq War, 2003–2011—Equipment and supplies—Juvenile literature. 3. Iraq War, 2003–2011—Transportation—Juvenile literature. 4. United States—Armed Forces—Equipment—Juvenile literature. 5. Iraq—Armed Forces—Equipment—Juvenile literature. I. Title.
UG615.F57 2014
956.7044'34—dc23 2013005531

Editorial Credits
Aaron Sautter, editor; Heidi Thompson, designer; Eric Manske, production specialist

Photo Credits
Alamy: Colin C. Hill, 21 (middle), Panzermeister, 23 (bottom), Troy GB images, 27 (top); DoD photo by MC2 Kevin S. O'Brien USN, 28b; Getty Images: AFP/Patrick Baz, 7, Scott Nelson, 4; Newscom: AFP/Getty Images/Essam Al-Sudani, 21t; Newscom: Dopson Flight Collection, 11b, EPA/Peter Oetzmann, 22b, Getty Images/AFP/Michael Dunlea, 17b, SR Flight Collection/GR Photography, 11t; U.S. Air Force photo, cover, 14b, A1C Jason Epley, 13b, Capt. Justin T. Watson, 9b, Master Sgt. Kevin J. Gruenwald, 12b, Paul Ridgeway, 14t, Staff Sgt. Bennie J. Davis III, 8, Staff Sgt. Derrick C. Goode, 10t, Staff SGt. Jason Robertson, 20b, Staff Sgt. John Houghton, 19b, Staff Sgt. Reynaldo Ramon, 15t, Staff Sgt. Robert Barney, 18t, Tech. Sgt. Richard Freeland, 9t; U.S. Army photo, 19t, Frank Trevino, 18b, Sgt. Jacob Smith, 22t, Spc. Jeffrey Alexander, 23t, Spc. Joshua E. Powell, 15b, Spc. Justin A. Naylor, 21b; U.S. Coast Guard photo by PA1 Tom Sperduto, 29t; U.S. Marine Corps photo by Cpl. Justin L. Wainscott, 16, Gunnery Sgt. Kevin W. Williams, 25t, Master Sgt. Christopher Matt, 20t, Sgt. Jason W. Fudge, 17t, Staff Sgt. Leo Salinas, 24; U.S. Navy Photo by JO1 Jeremy L. Wood, 12t, MC1 Anderson Bomjardim, 28t, MC2 John Stratton, 29b, MC2 Nikki Smith, 27b, PH1 Michael W. Pendergrass, 26t, PH1 Thomas Lynaugh, 27m, PH2 Daniel J. McLain, 13t, PH3 Angel Roman-Otero, 25b, PH3 Philip A. McDaniel, 10b, PHAN Rob Gaston, 26b

Artistic Effects
Shutterstock

Printed in the United States of America in Stevens Point, Wisconsin.
042013 007227WZF13

Table of Contents

Ch.1 > Operation Iraqi Freedom

It was the middle of the night on March 20, 2003. Planes and missiles streaked across the sky over Baghdad, Iraq. Explosions rocked the city. Meanwhile, lines of assault vehicles and tanks rumbled through the desert toward Baghdad. After months of build-up, Operation Iraqi Freedom had finally begun.

U.S. forces gathered in Kuwait to prepare for the invasion of Iraq in 2003.

U.S. leaders believed that Iraqi leader Saddam Hussein had chemical and biological weapons. They also thought Hussein was trying to build nuclear weapons. They were afraid Hussein could give these weapons to **terrorists** who wanted to harm the United States. In November 2002 the United Nations (U.N.) had ordered Hussein to give up his weapons. Meanwhile, U.S. President George W. Bush ordered the U.S. military to prepare for a possible invasion.

Over the next few months, Hussein continually refused to cooperate with U.N. weapons inspectors. Finally, on March 20, 2003, the United States and Great Britain led a **coalition** of 49 countries to invade Iraq and remove Hussein from power.

In less than two months, Iraq's major cities and ports had been captured. By May 1, President Bush announced an end to major combat. Saddam Hussein was later captured and jailed in December. Many people thought the war was over. But Iraqi **insurgents** continued to fight. The war dragged on for eight more years until its official end in December 2011.

terrorist—someone who uses violence and threats to frighten and harm people

coalition—an alliance of people, groups, or countries working together toward a common goal

insurgent—a person who rebels and fights against his or her country's ruling government and those supporting it

MILITARY MACHINES

The United States and Great Britain used the world's most advanced military vehicles during the Iraq War. Aircraft were especially important. Unmanned aerial vehicles (UAVs) used **Global Positioning Systems** (GPS) and advanced cameras to locate enemy targets. Stealth bombers and fighters attacked targets while avoiding Iraq's outdated **radar** systems. Ships and submarines launched guided missiles to hit targets hundreds of miles away.

Iraq had few planes or ships for defense. And most of Iraq's land vehicles were old and outdated vehicles from the former **Soviet Union**. Some Iraqi tanks had the firepower to damage U.S. and British tanks. But the coalition's armored vehicles were stronger and more advanced. Very few were damaged or destroyed during the early stages of the war.

However, Iraqi insurgents soon learned effective ways to fight back. They covered the country with homemade bombs called improvised explosive devices (IEDs). IEDs were often hidden on roads to blow up military vehicles as they drove by. The U.S. military responded by designing new vehicles that could survive the explosions.

Coalition forces used a variety of unmanned aerial vehicles to help find and fight Iraqi forces.

The war was costly. But the military's advanced vehicles helped bring a swift end to Hussein's grip on Iraq. Coalition forces and their vehicles helped bring a free and democratic government to the Iraqi people.

Global Positioning System—an electronic tool used to find the location of an object

radar—a device that uses radio waves to track the location of objects

Soviet Union—a former communist nation made up of 15 republics that included Russia, Ukraine, and other nations of eastern Europe and central Asia

Ch.2 Vehicles in the Air

Operation Iraqi Freedom began with a "shock and awe" campaign against Baghdad. The goal was to destroy Iraq's will to fight. Nonstop air strikes destroyed Hussein's palaces and many government buildings. Iraq had very few aircraft to stop the coalition forces. By the end of April 2003, more than 1,800 coalition aircraft had already seen action in the war.

•••BOMBERS•••

B-2 Spirit Stealth Bomber

These U.S. stealth bombers flew nonstop missions from Whiteman Air Force Base in Missouri to Baghdad. The 6,700 mile (10,800 kilometer) trip required midair refueling. The B-2's unique shape and special surface coating made it nearly invisible to enemy radar.

B-52 Stratofortress

On March 21, 2003, B-52s launched about 100 long-range cruise missiles on Baghdad. The Stratofortress bomber carried more types of weapons and ammunition than any other U.S. bomber. It could carry up to 70,000 pounds (31,750 kilograms) of bombs and missiles.

A-10 Thunderbolt II

Thunderbolts were equipped with night-vision systems. These U.S. attack aircraft flew many night missions as both bombers and fighters. Thunderbolts were heavily armed with various bombs and missiles. They also carried large 30 mm cannons.

WAR FACT

Coalition bombers could not have flown long missions to Iraq without refueling. KC-135 Stratotanker refueling planes could carry and transfer about 31,000 gallons (117,000 liters) of fuel in midair.

F-117A Nighthawk

F-117A Nighthawks led the first air attack over Baghdad. These U.S. stealth fighters carried laser-guided bombs and air-to-surface missiles. They were designed for night missions. Pilots relied on GPS and automated flight systems to fly the planes at night.

F/A-18 E Super Hornet

U.S. F/A-18 E Super Hornets launched off the USS *Abraham Lincoln* to attack ground targets and provide air defense. These single-seat planes traveled 1,370 miles (2,200 km) per hour and as high as 50,000 feet (15,000 meters). They could attack targets up to 1,275 miles (2,050 km) away.

Tornado GR4

British Tornado fighters targeted antiaircraft weapons around missile sites and runways. The Tornado usually carried smart bombs or cruise missiles. But it could also be equipped with Air Launched Anti-Radiation Missiles (ALARMs) to destroy enemy radar systems.

Harriers

Unlike most fighters, Harrier jets could take off and land vertically, similar to a helicopter. This ability allowed Harriers to land near battlefields with no runways. The planes could be quickly refueled to provide continuous support for ground troops. U.S. and British Harriers were armed with missiles, bombs, and heavy machine guns. Some were equipped with special cameras for **reconnaissance** missions.

reconnaissance—a mission to gather information about an enemy

UH-60 Black Hawks

Black Hawks were all-purpose helicopters for U.S. forces in Iraq. They flew stealth missions and carried troops and equipment. They even carried political leaders and celebrities who visited the troops. Black Hawks could transport up to 11 soldiers and their gear. Or they could carry a large howitzer with its crew and 30 rounds of ammunition.

AH-64 Apache Longbow

Apaches were the U.S. Army's heavy attack helicopters. These powerful choppers were armed with missiles, rockets, and chain guns. They could fly up to 2 ½ hours and attack targets up to 300 miles (480 km) away. In spite of their advanced abilities, Apaches weren't always successful. During a raid on March 24, 2003, 40 Apache choppers came under heavy attack. Iraqi Republican Guard soldiers shot down one of the helicopters and heavily damaged 30 others. The choppers were forced to retreat and give up on the mission.

Puma HCI

British forces used Pumas to transport troops to mission sites. These battlefield helicopters had a three-person crew and could carry 12 fully-equipped soldiers or 4,000 pounds (1,800 kg) of cargo. Pumas traveled 169 miles (270 km) per hour and flew up to 17,000 feet (5,180 m) high.

WAR FACT

During the war the coalition used aircraft to drop millions of leaflets about Hussein's cruelty over Iraq's cities. They hoped the leaflets would help gain the support of Iraq's people.

Mi-17

The Iraqi military used Soviet-built Mi-17 choppers. They could transport 30 troops or 20 wounded soldiers. These single-rotor helicopters were armed with missiles and bombs as well as guns. They also were used for **surveillance** and laying mines.

surveillance—the act of keeping very close watch on someone, someplace, or something

Predators and Reapers

Both the United States and Great Britain flew unmanned Predator aircraft in Iraq. RQ-1 Predators used lasers and cameras to scout an area for up to 24 hours. They then transmitted the locations of enemy targets to combat planes for missile strikes. The MQ-9 Reaper was an armed version of the Predator. It fired laser-guided missiles at ground targets, including suspected terrorist bases. Reapers flew up to 25,000 feet (7,620 m) and could fly through some sandstorms.

RQ-4 Global Hawk

U.S. Global Hawks were used to patrol borders, search for enemy land vehicles, and identify Iraqi mine sites. These unarmed UAVs flew long-range missions up to 8,700 miles (14,000 km) at 357 miles (575 km) per hour.

MQ-5B Hunter

U.S. forces used Hunter UAVs for reconnaissance and surveillance in Iraq. Hunters were also one of the first UAVs to be armed. The MQ-5B carried up to 500 pounds (227 kg) of bombs or missiles. It could fly up to 22,000 feet (6,700 m) and stay in the air for up to 15 hours.

RQ-11B Raven

The RQ-11B Raven looked and flew like a model airplane. It weighed less than 5 pounds (2.3 kg) and could be carried in a soldier's backpack. Soldiers launched these small planes by hand. They flew Ravens by remote control for up to 80 minutes for reconnaissance missions.

WAR FACT

The numbers and letters in an aircraft's name stand for its identity and purpose. For example, the RQ-4 Global Hawk has an "R" for reconnaissance. The "Q" stands for an unmanned craft. The "4" represents its place in a series of aircraft systems.

Ch.3 > Vehicles on Land

The coalition brought its toughest, most advanced ground vehicles to fight in Iraq. Tanks and howitzers provided heavy firepower for ground combat while missile launchers targeted Iraqi aircraft. The Iraqis had few high-tech vehicles. They often used simple pickup trucks or dump trucks to transport troops and supplies.

•••LIGHT INFANTRY VEHICLES•••

HMMWV (Humvee)

Humvees were the U.S. military's main transport vehicle. At the start of the war, these lightweight vehicles were unarmored and sat low to the ground. They were easy targets for IEDs. The Army later added stronger armor and bullet-resistant glass to make the vehicles safer for troops.

Mine Resistant Ambush Protected (MRAP) Vehicle

Humvees were eventually replaced with Mine Resistant Ambush Protected vehicles (MRAPs). These strongly armored vehicles had V-shaped hulls that could redirect the blast from roadside bombs. Two types of MRAPs were used in the war. Four-wheeled versions could transport 10 troops, while the six-wheeled type carried 16 soldiers.

Scimitar Armoured Reconnaissance Vehicle

The British Royal Armoured Corps used these small tracked vehicles in rough terrain. Scimitars were armed with machine guns and 30 mm cannons for defense. But their main purpose was reconnaissance work.

Patriot Missile Launching System (MIM-104)

The Patriot's radar system detected and tracked enemy planes up to 62 miles (100 km) away. The radar and launcher were mounted on a semitrailer and pulled by an armored truck. In Iraq the Patriot system was upgraded to use up to 16 missiles at a time.

WAR FACT

Patriot stands for Phased Array Tracking Intercept of Target.

Heavy Expanded Mobility Tactical Truck (HEMTT)

These massive U.S. trucks served different support roles in Iraq. HEMTT M983 tractors towed Patriot missile systems to launching sites. A HEMTT M985A4 guided missile transporter included a crane that could lift up to 5,400 pounds (2,500 kg) of missiles.

M270 Mulitple Launch Rocket System

This tracked surface-to-surface system could fire up to 12 rockets in less than a minute. When they reached their destination, the rockets dropped more than 600 bomblets on ground targets. The M270 traveled 40 miles (64 km) per hour on land.

Robot Warriors

Several types of remote-controlled robots helped keep coalition troops safe in Iraq. Dragon Runner robots were equipped with a video camera and a microphone. These tough robots could be thrown through windows, over walls, down stairs, or even out of moving trucks. Dragon Runners were designed to work regardless of how they landed. Soldiers used them to scout dangerous areas from a safe distance.

Fido was a bomb-sniffing robot used to search inside and under vehicles. Fido weighed 52 pounds (23.6 kg). Cameras and grippers were attached to the end of the robot's 7-foot (2.1-m) arm to pick up explosives.

Remote-controlled BomBots carried detonators to IEDs. After these small robots moved away, soldiers could explode the bombs safely. BomBots weighed just 15 pounds (6.8 kg) and were easy to transport.

M1A1 Abrams

The M1A1 Abrams was the primary tank for coalition troop protection and reconnaissance in Iraq. A four-person crew controlled this 67.6-ton (61.3-metric ton) giant. These U.S. tanks were heavily armored and carried a 120 mm gun. But enemy fighters still damaged these tanks with roadside bombs. They could also be damaged by rocket-propelled grenades aimed at the tank's tracks.

Bradley M2A3

U.S.-built Bradley infantry fighting vehicles were designed to transport troops and provide protection as they advanced into enemy territory. These tracked vehicles carried a 25 mm cannon, a missile system, and a 7.62 mm machine gun. Bradleys were crewed by a commander, a gunner, and a driver. They could carry six fully-equipped soldiers into battle. The M2A3 was equipped with several advanced computer systems to help the gunner accurately fire on enemy positions.

Challenger 2

This British battle tank was equipped with heat-sensing cameras and a day/night periscope. It was armed with a 120 mm gun, plus chain and machine guns. In 2003 the British 7th Armoured Brigade used Challenger tanks to capture the city of Basra and secure nearby oil fields.

AS90 Braveheart

The British self-propelled AS90 Braveheart howitzer had an automatic ammunition loading system. It could fire up to six rounds per minute. Its 155 mm gun could hit targets up to 15 miles (24 km) away.

M109A6 Paladin Howitzer

The self-propelled Paladin fired four rounds of ammunition per minute. Onboard computer systems allowed the Paladin to lock onto a target, load, and fire its weapon within 45 seconds. When loaded for battle, it weighed more than 63,000 pounds (28,500 kg).

T-72 Battle Tank

Iraqi forces used this Soviet-built tank early in the war. It featured an antiaircraft machine gun and a 125 mm gun. It weighed 45 tons (40.8 metric tons) and traveled 37 miles (60 km) per hour. It was powerful enough to destroy an M1 Abrams tank. However, Iraqi tank crews were not as well trained as coalition tank crews. They often did not use T-72 tanks effectively.

T-55 Battle Bank

Armed with a 100 mm cannon and machine gun, T-55s provided front line support for Iraqi troops. These Soviet-built tanks could be outfitted to cross water. However, T-55s were old and outdated. They often broke down and were not very effective in the war.

BMP Fighting Vehicle

Iraq's forces used this Soviet-built armored infantry vehicle on both land and water. The BMP held a crew of three and could transport eight soldiers. It was sometimes armed with a **turret**-mounted gun that fired missiles.

ZSU-23-4 "Shilka"

Iraqi forces also used the "Shilka" self-propelled antiaircraft vehicle. It carried four cannons and could fire up to 3,400 rounds per minute. A water system helped cool the rapid-fire guns. The Soviet-made Shilka got its nickname from Russia's Shilka River.

turret—a rotating armored structure that holds a weapon on top of a military vehicle

Ch.4 > Vehicles at Sea

Coalition forces used many ships during the war. Large warships launched fighter planes and cruise missiles to attack targets inside Iraq. Submarines patrolled the Persian Gulf and Red Sea. Smaller ships protected oil platforms and searched for underwater explosives. **Amphibious** assault vehicles (AAVs) carried troops from sea onto land to attack Iraq's ports.

•••AMPHIBIOUS ASSAULT VEHICLES•••

AAVP-7A1

U.S. Marines in AAVP-7A1 vehicles captured the Umm Qasr port on the second day of the invasion. These amphibious vehicles were often the first to land in a shore assault. They carried 21 Marines plus the crew and 10,000 pounds (4,540 kg) of cargo. They were armed with machine guns and grenade launchers.

amphibious—a vehicle or craft that can travel both over land and in water

LAV-25

LAV-25s carried a turret-mounted 25 mm cannon, two M240 machine guns, and two grenade launchers. Marines in LAV-25s destroyed Iraqi armored vehicles in the first firefight of the invasion. These vehicles could travel on inland waterways but were not designed to travel on the ocean.

Amphibious Assault Ship

U.S. Navy amphibious assault ships were 844 feet (260 m) long and looked like small aircraft carriers. Wasp-class assault ships were armed with missile launchers and machine guns. They also carried helicopters and AV-8B Harrier jets.

WAR FACT

The U.S. and British Navies include abbreviations in their ships' names. The British title HMS stands for "Her Majesty's Ship." USS stands for "United States Ship."

Aircraft Carriers

U.S. aircraft carriers traveled with support ships and submarines. Nimitz-class carriers were 1,092 feet (330 m) long. They carried more than 3,000 sailors and a 1,500-person air crew. These ships served as bases for multiple types of jets.

WAR FACT

Tomahawk cruise missiles traveled about 550 miles (885 km) per hour. They could strike ground targets 900 to 1,350 miles (1,448 to 2,173 km) away.

Los Angeles Submarines

Twelve Los Angeles-class submarines launched more than one-third of the Tomahawk cruise missiles fired on Iraq. These nuclear-powered submarines had 12 launch tubes and carried 143 sailors. The USS *Cheyenne* launched the first Tomahawk missile of the war.

Trafalgar Submarines

British Trafalgar-class submarines were used for reconnaissance and attack missions. They carried homing torpedoes used to target other submarines and surface ships. The British HMS *Turbulent* joined U.S. submarines to launch Tomahawk missiles into Iraq.

Destroyers

U.S. Arleigh Burke-class destroyers, like the USS *Milius*, often launched Tomahawk missiles during the war. These warships were 505 feet (154 m) long and traveled faster than 34 miles (55 km) per hour.

Frigates

Frigates were used to search for enemy submarines and served as landing platforms for helicopters. The British frigate HMS *Iron Duke* helped patrol oil platforms in the Persian Gulf. The ship was armed with surface-to-air missiles, machine guns, and torpedoes.

Mine Countermeasures Ships (MCMs)

Mine countermeasures ships hunted for underwater explosives. MCMs were 224 feet (68.3 m) long and armed with two .50-caliber machine guns. Using **sonar** and cameras, crews searched Iraqi harbors and river bottoms for underwater mines. They then triggered the explosives with remote-controlled mine-detonating equipment.

Small Unit Riverine Craft (SURC)

The U.S. Navy patrolled the Euphrates River with shallow-water riverine assault boats. These boats carried up to 28 people and traveled 40 miles (64 km) per hour. They were armed with multiple machine guns and a grenade launcher.

sonar—a device that uses sound waves to find underwater objects

Patrol Boats

U.S. Coast Guard patrol boats were equipped with advanced navigation and electronics systems. The 110-foot (34-m) USCGC *Adak* patrolled the Northern Arabian Gulf to protect oil platforms from terrorists.

Large Medium Speed Roll-on/Roll-off Ship (LMSR)

LMSR ships supported U.S. Navy operations by transporting heavy cargo to the Persian Gulf. The 951-foot (290-m) LMSR was the size of three football fields. These ships carried up to 58 tanks, 48 tracked vehicles, and 900 other wheeled vehicles. The USNS *Pililaau* transported armored trucks to Iraq from South Carolina.

WAR FACT

The Iraqis had few seaworthy ships. To lay underwater mines, they disguised tugboats and barges as oil carriers to sneak past coalition patrol boats.

Glossary

amphibious (am-FI-bee-uhs)—a vehicle or craft that can travel both over land and in water

coalition (koh-uh-LISH-uhn)—an alliance of people, groups, or countries working together toward a common goal

Global Positioning System (GLOH-buhl puh-ZI-shuh-ning SISS-tuhm)—an electronic tool used to find the location of an object

insurgent (in-SUR-juhnt)—a person who rebels and fights against his or her government and those supporting it

radar (RAY-dar)—a device that uses radio waves to track the location of objects

reconnaissance (ree-KAH-nuh-suhnss)—a mission to gather information about an enemy

sonar (SOH-nar)—a device that uses sound waves to find underwater objects; sonar stands for sound navigation and ranging

Soviet Union (SOH-vee-et YOON-yuhn)—a former communist nation made up of 15 republics that included Russia, Ukraine, and other nations of eastern Europe and central Asia

surveillance (suhr-VAY-luhnss)—the act of keeping very close watch on someone, someplace, or something

terrorist (TER-ur-ist)—someone who uses violence and threats to frighten and harm people

turret (TUR-it)—a rotating, armored structure that holds a weapon on top of a military vehicle

Read More

Peppas, Lynn. *Military Helicopters: Flying into Battle.* Vehicles on the Move. New York: Crabtree Pub. Co., 2012.

Simons, Lisa M. Bolt. *The Kids' Guide to Military Vehicles.* Kids' Guides. North Mankato, Minn.: Capstone Press, 2010.

Tougas, Shelley. *Weapons, Gear, and Uniforms of the Iraq War.* Equipped for Battle. North Mankato, Minn.: Capstone Press, 2012.

Internet Sites

FactHound offers a safe, fun way to find Internet sites related to this book. All of the sites on FactHound have been researched by our staff.

Here's all you do:

Visit *www.facthound.com*

Type in this code: 9781429699143

Check out projects, games and lots more at
www.capstonekids.com

Index